Find 10 hidden objects in the picture

Find 10 hidden objects in the picture

Find 10 hidden objects in the picture

04

Find 10 hidden objects in the picture

Find 10 hidden objects in the picture

Find 10 hidden objects in the picture

Find 10 hidden objects in the picture

Find 10 hidden objects in the picture

Find 14 hidden objects in the picture

Find 10 hidden objects in the picture

Find 10 hidden objects in the picture

Find 10 hidden objects in the picture

Find 11 hidden objects in the picture

Find 14 hidden objects in the picture

Find 10 hidden objects in the picture

Find 9 hidden objects in the picture

Find 10 hidden objects in the picture

Find 10 hidden objects in the picture

Find 10 hidden objects in the picture

Find 10 hidden objects in the picture

Find 10 hidden objects in the picture